THE KNOPF POETRY SERIES

ANTARCTIC TRAVELLER

ANTARCTIC TRAVELLER

Poems by Katha Pollitt

ALFRED A. KNOPF   NEW YORK   1982

THIS IS A BORZOI BOOK PUBLISHED BY ALFRED A. KNOPF, INC.

Published in the United States by Alfred A. Knopf, Inc., New York, and
simultaneously in Canada by Random House of Canada Limited, Toronto.
Distributed by Random House, Inc., New York.

Acknowledgment is gratefully given to the following magazines, in which some
of the poems in this book originally appeared:

Antaeus: "Parthians."
The Atlantic Monthly: "January Thaw," "Metaphors of Women," "Nettles,"
"Night Blooming Flowers," "Onion," "Potatoes," "Thinking of the World as
Idea," and "Two Fish."
Mademoiselle: "Not Your Kind of Weather," "Penelope Writes," and "When
We Drive at Night."
The Nation: "Intimation," "Man Across the Street," "A Turkish Story," and
"Woman Asleep on a Banana Leaf."
The New Yorker: "Archaeology," "Ballet Blanc," "Blue Window," "Composition
in Black and White," "A Discussion of the Vicissitudes of History Under a
Pine Tree," "Failure," "Moon and Flowering Plum," "To an Antarctic
Traveller," "Whose Sleeves?," and "Wild Orchids."
Paris Review: "Of the Scythians," "Seal Rock," and "Wild Escapes."
Pequod: "Turning Thirty."
Ploughshares: "In Horse Latitudes."
Poetry: "Eggplant," "November Fifth, Riverside Drive," "A Screen Depicting
the 54 Episodes of the Tale of Genji on a Background of Gold Leaf,"
"Sea Grasses," and "Tomato."
Shenandoah: "Chinese Finches."

"Blue Window," "In Horse Latitudes," and "A Turkish Story" also appeared in
The Ardis Anthology of New American Poetry (Ardis, 1977) .

Library of Congress Cataloging in Publication Data
Pollitt, Katha.   Antarctic traveller.
    Poems.   I. Title.
PS3566.0533 A82   811'.54   81–47521
ISBN 0–394–52004–1   AACR2
ISBN 0–394–74895–6 (pbk.)

Manufactured in the United States of America

FIRST EDITION

In memory of my mother
Leanora Levine Pollitt

I wish to express my gratitude to the Ingram Merrill Foundation and Creative Artists in Public Service, and to the Robert Frost Place in Franconia, New Hampshire, where some of these poems were written.

I am grateful to my father, to Belle, Joe, and Mima, and to all my family, for much loving interest in the progress of this book.

I would also like to thank Daniel Zitin, for his insightful criticism and boundless encouragement.

CONTENTS

I

II   Five Poems from Japanese Paintings

III

~~~

The use of this symbol indicates a
stanza break at the bottom of the page.

"It may be that the gulfs will wash us down:
It may be we shall touch the Happy Isles,
And see the great Achilles, whom we knew."

I

BLUE WINDOW

That longing you have to be invisible,
transparent as glass, thin air—
that is what moves you certain times to tears
watching the evening fill with city lights
and the long dusty summer avenues
rise weightless through the air
and tremble like constellations in a sky
so deep and clear you are your one desire,
Oh, let me be that blue . . .

It is your other, solitary self
that calls you to the window where you stand
dreaming in the dusk in an ecstasy of longing
while your white apartment full of plants and pictures
grows strange with shadows, as though under water.
And in another moment
you would stream out the window and into the sky like a breath—
but it is almost too dark to see. In the next apartment
a door is flung open. Someone speaks someone's name.

NOT YOUR KIND OF WEATHER

This clear day comes like a letter from America
or a gift of big glass bells.

All morning the sun
clanged on the roof and the high impossible clouds
created themselves out of nothing.
I think of palaces,
their windows brilliant with frost
or girls in blue hats
crossing the Pont de l'Alma like a procession of irises.
I say, Amaze me, amaze me:
these boulevards are streaming.
I move through the light like light.

This is not your weather at all.
You loved the ambiguous,
the half-light at five o'clock.
Uncertainty made you strong.
Thinking of you, I cannot trust this day:

somehow you are here, you dominate even this city
like a fault in the street, a black seed
in the absolute blue of the sky
or the mad concierge:
down in the courtyard she twists to the leaves she rakes,
her black contrapuntal figure
a crow
a terror.

IN HORSE LATITUDES

What does the sea want, my clothes, my keys, my face?
This is the mind's Sargasso,
expansive as Kansas flatlands, the big dead place.

The weeds stir, they make promises. I'm light as a shell.
Immobile, the sea bottom
glints at my emptiness with ship's tackle, jewels,

railway tickets, photographs: the blue-eyed platoons
grinning up from their doomed jungles.
I am left with nothing to hold, nothing to do

but imagine those horses the Spaniards abandoned here:
at night I have seen them rise
to graze the glassy prairie and whinny their fear.

Anxious, disconsolate,
they sniff for a wind. Sour water drips down their tails.
Ghost horses, I am like you. When the gray line of a sail

nicks the horizon, my heart strains forward too:
heavy with salt, the blood
leans like a tide, but has no place to go.

The Horse Latitudes are a region of unusual calm in the North
Atlantic Ocean. When sailing ships were becalmed there, cargo and
horses would be thrown overboard. Thus lightened, the ship could
take advantage of whatever wind there might be.

OF THE SCYTHIANS

who came whirling out of the North
like a locust swarm, storm-darkening the sky,
their long hair whipping in the wind like the manes of horses,
no one remembers anything now but I:

how they screamed to the slaughter, as the skirl of a thousand flutes
fashioned from enemies' thighbones shrilled them on.
Naked they rode. We stood by our huts, stunned mute:
gold flashed from each spear, gold glittered on each arm.

I was a child in the temple. The old priest
hid me in a secret cellar with the images.
Above my head I heard him chant a last
prayer to the god. Since then

I scorn to mix with those who have come after.
Fat farmers, milky scribblers! What do they know
who have never heard the Scythians' terrible laughter
or seen in the wind their glittering wild hair flow?

PARTHIANS

"For the Parthians threw their darts as they fled . . .
and it is, indeed, a cunning practice."—Plutarch

Dust and gray dunes. Ribbed bed of an ancient sea.
What do the black birds cry who roost in these thorns?

For years we have tracked you
by evidence of your absence:

a gold ring caught on a branch, a charred
kitchen of stones that says, last night you were here.

Old ones,
empty-handed in the blue

horizon's freedom, that dull rubbish you
walked off from is our fate.

Wait
for us. Speak to us.

Each night we sleep
in your camp of the night before

and dream of pitched battle:
that gash and grapple, how we promise to love it,

~~~

it would be an embrace, it would be a way of knowing.
But we are trapped in your past,

the arrows that destroy us
float casually backward, as at a foolish regret,

and a new morning heats its terrible metals.
Yet we go on,

we go on,
as though if we could just move fast enough

we'd break through the flaw in time
that keeps us locked in parallel dimensions.

Beautiful mirages! In the distance
glimmer what green oases, what cool leaves?

Your tents stand shimmering, as though seen through water.

FAILURE

You'd never set foot in this part of town before,
so how could the landlady wink as if she recognized you?
Still, it's uncanny, the way when you open the door
to your room the scratched formica bureau and table
give off a gleam of welcome, the foldaway bed
sags happily into itself like an old friend,
and look, the previous tenant has considerately
left you his whole library: *Ferns of the World*
and *How to Avoid Probate*. Even the water stain
spreading on the ceiling has your profile.

Well, never mind. Unpack your suitcase, put
boric acid out for the roaches. Here
too there are plenty of tears for things, probably, but
don't think about that just now. Outside your window
ailanthus trees, bringing you an important message
about the nutritive properties of garbage,
wave their arms for attention, third-world raiders,
scrawny, tough, your future if you're lucky.

A TURKISH STORY

The rugweaver kept his daughters at home, unmarried.
The soft clash of their bangles said *wish for us, wish.*

Longing for a son, a handsome agronomist,
for years he worked on a rug that would have no errors:

the blue was disappointment, the red was rancor.
His daughters circled their eyes with kohl and went to the market,

they stirred pots, singing
a song about a lion asleep under an almond tree.

When he died each married a husband strong as the sea.
They danced on the rug and its errors blazed like stars.

MAN ACROSS THE STREET

All of your neighbors were wearing gray felt hats.
You went out and bought a gray felt hat.
I remember your eyes like the sea
the color of no color.

The sea also is lonely
taking into its bed
bottles, love letters, shoes.
How it loves feeling over and over
whatever hands have touched.

The sea pleads with the land
it says hold me, hold me.
You ache to be included
in subways, the dark theater

and like a tide
you comfort yourself with boredom:
look at your room
the swept floor, the bare table.

And yet the sea can rage.
It knows what it wants

its treasure, its gold daughter.
You have forgotten
what long ago you left
in a drawer in a room somewhere.

Listen to the waves, how they keep crying
grief, grief.
All night you lie awake and try to remember.

IN MEMORY

"But can we not sometimes speak of a darkening
  (for example) of our memory-image?"—Wittgenstein

Over the years, they've darkened, like old paintings
or wainscotting in a damp house in the country,
until now the streets where you roller-skated brim with twilight,
your mother drinks morning coffee from a cup of shadows,
and out in the garden, the hardest August noon
is washed with a tender, retrospective blue—
like woodsmoke, or the shade of an unseen lilac.
Upstairs, you can hardly make yourself out, a child
peering out the window, speechless with happiness,
reciting your future in an endless summer dusk.

At first, this maddened you. You wanted to see
your life as a rope of diamonds: permanent, flashing.
Strange, then, how lately this darkening of memory moves you,
as though what it claimed it also made more true,
the way discoloring varnish on a portrait
little by little engulfs the ornate background—
the overstuffed sofa, the velvet-and-gold festoons
framing an elegant vista—but only deepens
the calm and serious face. The speaking eyes.

PENELOPE WRITES

In my house there's a place for everything:
a shelf for the blue cups, one for the cups with flowers,
a box for bits of string—

Oh, I was wild to order
years like knives in a drawer!

Now these dark larders,
cupboards, chests, confuse and frighten me.
A loud, unappeasable anger

wastes in them and rattles like a sea.
I keep them locked. Husband, on your long oceans
islands rise up to save you, sudden, blue,

miraculous as dolphins.
And each time you think, "Why not? I'm young! I'm young!
It is right that such things happen."

While I—not young
or beautiful,
an ordinary woman—

why should I care if you come back after all?
For years
I've sat at the window, those men at the kitchen table.

~~~

Don't ask me why I scheme
to keep this lie. My neighbors crowd to see
the ingenious work appearing on my loom,

a man and wife posing so decorously,
so sweetly among roses. No one imagines
how almost lovingly

with what delight each night I make destruction.
I rip and slash. My fingers bleed. And then
I dream in my abandon
I am tearing my whole house down.

TURNING THIRTY

This spring, you'd swear it actually gets dark earlier.
At the elegant new restaurants downtown
your married friends lock glances over the walnut torte:
it's ten o'clock. They have important jobs
and go to bed before midnight. Only you
walking alone up the dazzling avenue
still feel a girl's excitement, for the thousandth time
you enter your life as though for the first time,
as an immigrant enters a huge, mysterious capital:
Paris, New York. So many wide plazas, so many marble addresses!
Home, you write feverishly
in all five notebooks at once, then faint into bed
dazed with ambition and too many cigarettes.

Well, what's wrong with that? Nothing, except
really you don't believe wrinkles mean character
and know it's an ominous note
that the Indian skirts flapping on the sidewalk racks
last summer looked so gay you wanted them all
but now are marked clearer than price tags: not for you.
Oh, what were you doing, why weren't you paying attention
that piercingly blue day, not a cloud in the sky,

when suddenly "choices"
ceased to mean "infinite possibilities"
and became instead "deciding what to do without"?
No wonder you're happiest now
riding on trains from one lover to the next.
In those black, night-mirrored windows
a wild white face, operatic, still enthralls you:
a romantic heroine,
suspended between lives, suspended between destinations.

CHINESE FINCHES

Their housewarming present to themselves
hung in a bamboo cage between
the philodendron and Boston fern
and hid a sort of cabbagy ooze
from somebody's drain. That was the year
he papered the wall with Roland Barthes
and shrieked, when he'd had a Scotch or four,
"I *am* contemporary literature!"
Her mother called each night at one.

She dreamed of blood. *And in Shanghai*
the young bride tucks her tiny feet
under her luck-embroidered gown
and thinks of dynasties of rice
plump, immaculate, bagged tight
in gleaming jars on the storeroom shelves
and wonders why she feels so sad.
Her horoscope says: sons. So these
coy darters chittered on their perch

deaf as golden lotuses
or carp in an ornamental pond
to tears or slamming doors or shouts
as winter dawn crept back again
to blanch the gay Design Research
pillows to ash on the borrowed couch.
Let love go down to disarray,

they sipped their water peaceably
and nibbled the seed in their spoonsize manger

for all the world small citizens
still of that practical, prosperous land
where the towns sleep safe in the Emperor's hand
and fields yield fruit and women sons
and red means wealth and never danger
and even the thief hung up by his thumbs
bares black snaggle teeth with a sort of pride
to demonstrate for the watching crowd
to what swift grief all folly comes.

BALLET BLANC

Baryshnikov leaps higher than your heart
in the moonlit forest, center stage, and pleads
with the ghostly corps, who pirouette, gauzed white
and powdered blue, like pearls, the star Sylphides

of Paris, 1841. You swoon
back in red plush. Oboes, adagio,
sing *love is death*—but death's this lustrous queen
who twirls forever on one famous toe

while hushed in shadows, tier on golden tier
swirls to apotheosis in the ceiling.
Miles away, through clouds, one chandelier
swings dizzily. What feeling

sweeps you? Dinner's roses and tall candles,
a certain wine-flushed face, your new blue dress
merge with the scented crush of silks and sables—
through which, you're more and more aware, two eyes

stroke, meltingly, your neck. You glow, you sway,
it's as though the audience were dancing too
and with a last, stupendous tour jeté
turned for a solo suddenly to *you*

and you become the Duke, the Queen, Giselle,
and waltz in a whirl of white through the painted grove,

your gestures as extravagant as tulle,
as wild as nineteenth-century hopeless love,

as grand as bravo! and brava! On wings,
you splurge and take a taxi home instead.
The park looms rich and magical. It's spring,
almost. You float upstairs and into bed

and into dreams so deep you never hear
how all night long that witch, your evil fairy,
crows her knowing cackle in your ear:
Tomorrow you will wake up ordinary.

ARCHAEOLOGY

"Our real poems are already in us
  and all we can do is dig."—Jonathan Galassi

You knew the odds on failure from the start,
that morning you first saw, or thought you saw,
beneath the heatstruck plains of a second-rate country
the outline of buried cities. A thousand to one
you'd turn up nothing more than the rubbish heap
of a poor Near Eastern backwater:
a few chipped beads,
splinters of glass and pottery, broken tablets
whose secret lore, laboriously deciphered,
would prove to be only a collection of ancient grocery lists.
Still, the train moved away from the station without you.

How many lives ago
was that? How many choices?
Now that you've got your bushelful of shards
do you say, *give me back my years*
or wrap yourself in the distant
glitter of desert stars,
telling yourself it was foolish after all
to have dreamed of uncovering

some fluent vessel, the bronze head of a god?
Pack up your fragments. Let the simoom
flatten the digging site. Now come
the passionate midnights in the museum basement
when out of that random rubble you'll invent
the dusty market smelling of sheep and spices,
streets, palmy gardens, courtyards set with wells
to which, in the blue of evening, one by one
come strong veiled women, bearing their perfect jars.

THE DANCERS

So what if Sweeney buys drinks for Rachel Rabinowitz
or Aunt Helen's footman dandles the second parlormaid?
At the rank-and-file Greek furworkers' dinner
at Dante Caterers in Astoria last night
the floor was covered with iridescent vinyl
and the chandeliers were plastic and everyone spoke bad English
and said what a beautiful party
while to the electrified mandolins
of Athanasios and his Ethnorhythmics
the heavy-breasted, lacquered and mascaraed women
arose in their nylon dresses
of chemical turquoise, orange, and shocking pink
and danced with their dapper husbands
the foxtrot, the rhumba, and the lovely dances of Sparta
and did not profane them.

NOVEMBER FIFTH,
RIVERSIDE DRIVE

The sky a shock, the ginkgoes yellow fever,
I wear the day out walking. November, and still
light stuns the big bay windows on West End
Avenue, the park brims over with light like a bowl
and on the river
a sailboat quivers like a white leaf in the wind.

How like an eighteenth-century painting, this
year's decorous decline: the sun
still warms the aging marble porticos
and scrolled pavilions past which an old man,
black-coated apparition of Voltaire,
flaps on his constitutional. "Clear air,
clear mind"—as if he could outpace
darkness scything home like a flock of crows.

THINKING OF THE WORLD
AS IDEA

1.

At three o'clock in the morning
the Staten Island ferry sails for pure joy.
Look: it is Bishop Berkeley's stateliest image
slipping its berth, moving out into the open harbor
beneath its lights nothing at all.

2.

You too amaze me, houses of Brooklyn.
All day you are meek, you cup
unhappiness like water
when all you want is to be nothing but windows,
to take off into the sky like a flock of birds.
Now the men sleep
who sat on the stoop after supper
and the woman who kept crying
"I don't care if I ever see you again"
and tenuous, luminous
you sway to the breath of that sleeper
who dreams the word that widens
until it becomes the world.

II

FIVE POEMS
FROM JAPANESE PAINTINGS

WILD ORCHIDS

"An anecdote has it that Tesshū painted orchids
 almost every day with a kind of religious
 fervor."—Museum catalogue

At the foot of a rock, bamboo and orchids,
small furled flowers that hold themselves aloof
from the mist that is everywhere.
You have left newspapers, indolent
quarrels over Sunday-morning coffee
to come to the museum with your lover
and admire these swirls
swept onto paper by an old monk
in less than ten minutes six hundred years ago
depicting the orchid,
which signifies the virtues of the noble man:
reticence, calm, clarity of mind.

WHOSE SLEEVES?

"Paintings entitled 'Whose Sleeves?' were studies of women's
   clothing and other possessions. The title implies a woman who
   is absent and missed, since beautiful clothes were thought to
   evoke the image of a beautiful woman and the fragrance
   arising from her kimono."—Museum catalogue

They keep her things exactly as she left them,
her heavy kimonos neatly draped on the rack:
the one with peacocks, the gold brocade,
the embroidered silk he bought her for special occasions.
On the floor, her koto and lacquered love-letter box,
a few fans, gifts from lovers.
One day in a cup of tea
she glimpsed her own top-heavy elaborate self
and laughed out loud. Her guests,
flustered from pompous compliments, promptly fled,
and so did not see her later
slipping away in nothing but her long black hair,
giddy as a child, aimless,
her pale skin shining faintly in the dusk
as she glided between dark trees
and across the bridge, where the moon was seen to be rising.
Like the moon she grew distant and smaller and brighter.
When she reached the horizon, she disappeared.

A SCREEN DEPICTING THE 54 EPISODES OF THE TALE OF GENJI ON A BACKGROUND OF GOLD LEAF

Everything happens at once: court ladies pick iris,
nobles hunt pheasant, poets walk in the snow.
In a dragon-prowed boat, under a canopy of flowers,
Prince Genji, the great lover,
sails in triumph from bedroom to bedroom: in each
a woman flutters like a tiny jewelled fan.

A tea merchant of Kyoto commissioned this screen for his wife.
At night as they lay on their uncomfortable mats
she stared at it and sighed.
He, however, concluded
that the difference between his own life and Prince Genji's
was that his lacked an artist
to blot discreetly all but fifty-four moments
with a dazzle of golden clouds.

MOON AND FLOWERING PLUM

A huge moon rises behind branches
stippled with white plum flowers, cold and frail,
like snow in early spring. Suddenly
it is that moment you have longed for,
you overflow like a cup,
like the moon overflowing with whiteness.
Could you live like that,
moving from incandescence to incandescence
as courtly viewers of plum flowers
proceed from one white orchard to the next?
Or would you find
their formal robes too stiff, the moon too slow,
the orchards, when you reached them,
muddy and full of frogs?

A DISCUSSION OF
THE VICISSITUDES OF HISTORY
UNDER A PINE TREE

The moment is what moves us, after all:
as here, in Taiga's painting,
the smoke-colored sky
swells like a breath, gentle,
already full of evening,
and the mountains, rounded by mist or distance,
rise like the natural
completion of a thought.
The light is a neutral fact of November or February,
a calm between weathers.

Under a pine, two old friends consider
vanished cities, conquests. Think of it,
all those horses: dust. And the men who rode them.
One speaks of last year's leaves,
dry stalks
rattling in the withered field;
the other gestures
to the usual changeless emblems:
pine, sky, mountain . . .

And what is there to say?
The truth is, neither
can really believe this has happened to him,

~~~

that he, who recalls the precise
glance of light and each sharp leaf
in a garden glimpsed on a back street fifty years ago,
has become someone else
who sits
in a bare field watching the slow
late glow of afternoon
tinge with faintest rose the monochromatic
landscape of an ambiguous season:

hills neither gray nor green,
sky neither blue nor gray.

III

VEGETABLE POEMS

1. Potatoes

Blind knobby eyes feeling out
the chinks in the damp black earth
all summer long these tunnel under the fence
to throttle the open field of milkweed and Queen Anne's lace
or live for years in cellars
their softened, mealy flesh
rotting into the earth, indistinguishable from earth
but still flinging up roots and occasional leaves
white as fish in caves.
Feel them, the swollen sac
the baggy elephant skin:
if they are edible, it is only by accident.

2. Tomato

It is the female fruit: the plush
red flesh the fat
sac of seeds and oh
those silky membranes
plump and calm
it fits your palm just so
it is that perfect softball of your childhood
the one you always lost
you can stroke the sleek skin
you can thumb
the comfortable curve beneath:
here's
all soft gum
no sheer
secret murderous teeth.

3. Onion

The smoothness of onions infuriates him
so like the skin of women or their expensive clothes
and the striptease of onions, which is also a disappearing act.
He says he is searching for the ultimate nakedness
but when he finds that thin green seed
that negligible sprout of a heart
we could have told him he'd only be disappointed.
Meanwhile the onion has been hacked to bits
and he's weeping in the kitchen most unromantic tears.

4. Eggplant

Like a dark foghorn in the yellow kitchen
we imagine the eggplant's
melancholy bass
booming its pompous operatic sorrows
a prince down on his luck
preserving among peasants
an air of dignified, impenetrable gloom
or Boris, dying,
booming, *I still am Tsar.*

5. Nettles

Like neighbors not invited to the wedding
these show up anyway: fat stalks
dull hairy leaves
they stand at the edge of the garden and cry *I burn!*
Ugly, but tenacious,
they make themselves useful: in teas,
poultices, cures for baldness and rheumatic complaints.
From us, such homely uses are all they can hope for,
but they too have their dream:
to be the chosen food of their beautiful loves
the peacock
small tortoiseshell
and red admiral caterpillars.

THERE

"Sometimes I seem to see a difficulty, but then again,
  I don't see a difficulty."—Gottlob Frege, when asked
  if he really believed that numbers were objects

Watch out. Here everything
has edges. You
could slit your thumb on a cloud.
Moments and shadows

sheer suddenly off
like cliffs
vertiginous
all glitter, all

obsidian. Words
fall like rocks at your feet
and stay there.
Look, already

the mockingbird that sang
so carelessly
since dawn outside our window
has littered the air

~~~

with glass
splinters, our least breath
hones six sides on our skin.
It's a blizzard, it's

an avalanche!
When the search party
finds us, will they guess
what ideal crystallizations

trapped us here?
Mirrors
flashing each other
back and forth forever:

diamonds that cut
diamonds.

INTIMATION

It says what you've always known
even as a child
when your grandmother sat on your bed in the dark
and sang that tuneless song
about a white goat and raisins and almonds
and you felt suddenly strange:
as though you had waked in the night and snow was falling.

COMPOSITION
IN BLACK AND WHITE

All day long they have sat here
black monosyllables, crows on a bare tree
while the hills slowed under snow,
becoming the fields, and the fields,
their sodden stubble of wheat
blanked over, leaned toward earth.

My heart rejoices as it can
and finds haphazard grace
in any mobile thing: I praise
these heavy fields, but more
the abrupt rising of crows
who flew up with a cry, their brilliant blacks
astonishing the air
as they scattered
leaving each branch sprung
taut, alive like wires.

SEA GRASSES

They feed no flocks. Bread
flailed from their meagre kernels
would starve out even an anchorite
if any tried
to force these idle flats to a spiritual purpose.
At Stonington, at Sea Bright,
they stand, not waiting,
only swaying a little in the wind,
as though to be a fact
among other facts—
to reflect their one particular
shade of pale yellowish green,
along with clouds and whatever occasional bird
happens to fly over,
into a transient pool
that the tide will shortly come back for—
in some sense, if not ours, should be enough.

WOMAN ASLEEP ON A BANANA LEAF

from a Chinese painting

Who wouldn't want such a bed?
In the heat of the afternoon, in a private shade,
she has hidden herself away
like a long, translucent, emerald-spotted snake
her skin a ripple, her spine
curved against the long green spine of this leaf.
Now let the ladies call from their silk pavilion,
and let Lord X compare someone else's skin
to the petals of peonies and other
appropriate seasonal flowers.
She dreams of skin that is cool and green and secret.
When she wakes up she will be completely happy.

JANUARY THAW

It began slowly. At first we could not hear
the small knock of water
come back from the deep places.
We had gone deaf with cold.
Now we wake and the streets
are water running to water
while overnight the fields have come down from the hills:
slow cows, earth-red and steamy,
they stand around our houses
and allow themselves to be touched.

I feel a light mist lift
on the wind when the wind rises.
On the pond the round ice floats free:
a moon
gone black in black water.

WHEN WE DRIVE AT NIGHT

When we drive at night
the houses shy away from the roads
or else they huddle together
confused, in the empty spaces.
The rush of so much longing is what they fear.

We ache when we drive
like the smashed Mack truck, abandoned by the side of the road,
which flashes its one red blinker
and continues to shriek for help: I want! I want!
From the dumps the tires are calling
softly, like mouths, in the rain.

And there are lives like this.
In our cars late at night, we are bigamists, nervous and aging,
saddened by wives.
We become that bus driver
who started out after lunch and drove to Nicaragua.

Who knows what we wish?
Watching you drive beside me,
I think of all the dark windows of automobiles,
the children asleep in the back,
and I picture the mind, unknown,

as hidden in caverns of the body
as the ghosts in these machines.

All night our eyes are full
of small black shadows on roads
that trail off into the back country and are lost.

WILD ESCAPES

"Escape: a cultivated plant run wild."
—*Webster's New Collegiate Dictionary*

Every night they went a little farther.
Restless, too hot to sleep
under the too-bright quilts she had made as a girl
the farmer's wife imagined she could hear them
slipping away like daughters
over the rough stone wall,
across the pasture, onto the lonely hills.
And nothing stayed:
the stars wheeled from her window,
the great pines waited, black, at the edge of the field,
and even these flowers, familiar
delicate umbels and traceries,
Queen Anne's lace, brought all the way from England,
refused to comfort her, preferred
to flaunt themselves in every ragged ditch,
lie down on bare cold stone—
as though in this raw air
a darker seed
drove on a starker, more essential white.

TWO FISH

Those speckled trout we glimpsed in a pool last year
you'd take for an image of love: it too should be
graceful, elusive, tacit, moving surely
among half-lights of mingled dim and clear,
forced to no course, of no fixed residence,
its only end its own swift elegance.
What would you say
if you saw what I saw the other day:
that pool heat-choked and fevered where sick blue
bubbled green scum and blistered water lily?
A white like a rolled-back eye or fish's belly
I thought I saw far out—but doubtless you
prefer to think our trout had left together
to seek a place with less inclement weather.

METAPHORS OF WOMEN

What if the moon
was never a beautiful woman?
Call it a shark shearing across black water.
An ear. A drum in a desert.
A window. A bone shoe.

What if the sea
was discovered to have no womb?
Let it be clouds, blue as the day they were born.
A ceremony of bells and questions.
A toothache. A lost twin.

What if a woman
is not the moon or the sea?
Say map of the air. Say green parabola.
Lichen and the stone that feeds it.
No rain. Rain.

NIGHT BLOOMING FLOWERS

In the vacant lot behind the hospital
where rainbeaten trash, smashed bottles, gutted bedsprings
sprawl in a flyblown drowse among cinders and slag

how suddenly
dusk takes on strangeness that is more
than blue air and the blue

transient aspect of things.
Look at the ground now, how it pales and glows
as one by one, night wakers—

catchfly, dame's violet, evening lychnis—
petal by petal unfold their secret hearts
and lift to the moon a whiteness like the moon.

Why does such candor move me
more than these failed acres?
I have cherished my refusals,

I have loved them
as if they were love. I stand,
as in the nineteenth-century photograph

the women of the house, four generations
in formal black, as for a great reception,
stood breathless, hushed in the shadowy conservatory

~~~

while under its glass dome
the night blooming cereus
strained its whole being to an inward rhythm

stiffened its thick stalk
and pulsed out its one flower
huge, fleshy, heavy-scented, glowing, green . . .

and later little Alice Emmeline
was carried upstairs by her father, half asleep,
not understanding what it was she'd seen
but trusting it, a mystery that would keep.

SEAL ROCK

They won't come to you. These nights, you could sit for a year
on the dock behind Arthur's Gift Shop and General Store
before you'd spot with your flashlight
a single silk-backed bather
nosing the trash fish dumped off the lobster boats,
lured to your human light from the night-black water.

Those visits, if they ever took place, ended long ago,
though the fishermen did no harm
to the silver-furred luck-bearing ones
who kept the cold caves we left and the waves no squall
spills the green-glass fullness of—
and even half-believed the old tales:

how they floated this drowner, nudged that skiff off rocks.
We bore them, perhaps. Or simply, their minds are elsewhere.
At any rate no girl
has married their king in centuries,
no sailor learned any secret from them worth shipwreck.

And yet, as the holiday ferry
smacks its smart salt-stiffened flags in the wind
we lean like children over the side: to lee
gleams the craggy castle to which they've withdrawn.
Huge, simple, sleek as Maillol bronzes, they

sprawl in the sun, or powerfully dive
and surface jewelled with spray

then lumber with heavy grace back up to their mates.
They are historyless, at peace. As our boat chuffs by,
the wind floats back fish stench
and a gabble of barks, sharp cries
that remind you of nothing but gulls or the creaking of rope.
They are no Sirens, we only weekend trippers.
Whatever their language, they are not speaking to us.

TO AN ANTARCTIC TRAVELLER

for Katherine Bouton

1.

When you return from the country of Refusal,
what will you think of us? Down there, No was final,
it had a glamor: so Pavlova turns,
narcissus-pale and utterly self-consumed,
from the claque, the hothouse roses; so the ice
perfects its own reflection, cold Versailles,
and does not want you, does not want even Scott,
grinding him out of his grave—Splash! off he goes,
into the ocean, comical, Edwardian,
a valentine thrown out. Afternoons
in the pastry shop, coffee and macaroons,
gossip's two-part intricate inventions
meshed in the sugary air like the Down and Across
of an endless Sunday puzzle—
what will such small temporizations mean
to you now you've travelled half the world and seen
the ego glinting at the heart of things?
Oh, I'm not worried, I know you'll come back
full of adventures, anecdotes of penguins
and the pilot who let you fly the cargo—but
you'll never be wholly ours. As a green glass bottle
is mouthed and rolled and dragged by the sea until
it forgets its life entirely—wine, flowers, candles,
the castaway's *save me* meticulously
printed in eleven languages—and now
it rests on the beach-house mantel

opalescent, dumb:
you'll stand at the cocktail party
among the beige plush furniture and abstracts,
and listen politely, puzzled, a foreigner
anxious to respect our customs but not quite
sure of the local dialect, while guests
hold forth on their love of travel—
and all the time you hear
the waves beat on that shore for a million years
go away   go away   go away
and the hostess fills your glass and offers crackers.

2.

They named a mountain after you down there.
Blank and shining, unclimbable,
no different from a hundred nameless others,
it did not change as you called to it from the helicopter
it was your name that changed
spinning away from you round and around and around
as children repeat a word
endlessly until at last it comes up pure
nonsense, hilarious. It smashed
and lay, a shattered mirror
smiling meaninglessly up at you from the unmarked snow.

More lasting than bronze is the monument I have raised
boasted Horace, not accurately, and yet
what else would we have him think? Or you,

that day you wrote yourself on the world itself
and as the pilot veered away forever
saw mist drift over your mountain almost immediately
and your name stayed behind
a testament of sorts, a proof of something
though only in the end white chalk
invisibly scribbled on a white tabula rasa.

A Note About the Author

Katha Pollitt was born in New York City, where she now lives.
She was educated at Radcliffe College and Columbia University,
and she has been the recipient of numerous grants and awards
for her poetry—among them the Robert Frost Award and
the Discovery Award offered by *The Nation* and the Poetry
Center of the 92nd Street Y in New York.

A Note on the Type

The text of this book was set on the Linotype in a type face called
Baskerville. The face is a facsimile reproduction of types cast from
molds made for John Baskerville (1706–75) from his designs.
The punches for the revived Linotype Baskerville were cut
under the supervision of the English printer George W. Jones.
John Baskerville's original face was one of the forerunners of
the type style known as "modern face" to printers—a "modern"
of the period A.D. 1800.

Composed by American–Stratford Graphic Services, Brattleboro, Vermont
Printed and bound by American Book–Stratford Press,
Saddle Brook, New Jersey

Typography and binding design by Virginia Tan